Noisy Jungle

Written by Lisa Thompson
Paintings by Ritva Voutila

Pebble was making some noise.
She hummed and growled.

River tried to be noisier.
He shouted loudly.

Pebble made more noise.
She banged and thumped on
a drum.

River tried to be even noisier.
He howled loudly.

Pebble made more noise.
She thumped and clanged on
the pots and pans.

River tried to be much noisier.
He screeched loudly.

Pebble made more noise.
She whistled and screeched on her blow horn.

River tried to be noisier still.
He screamed as loudly as he could.

"Quiet!" roared Rex.

"Not another sound! It's time for both of you to be quiet."

River and Pebble sat quietly in the tree house.

They were both too scared to make a sound.

They were so quiet they heard sounds they had never heard before.

And they saw creatures they had never seen!